D1081110

CONSOLIDATION

AN EFFECTIVE PROCESS FOR MAKING DISCIPLES

CLAUDIA DE FAJARDO

INTERNATIONAL CHARISMATIC MISSION
SANTAFÉ DE BOGOTA D.C. COLOMBIA
2001

2000 © Claudia de Fajardo

All rights reserved. No part of this publication may be reproduced, stored in a retrieval system or transmitted in any form or by any means, electronic, mechanical, photocopying or otherwise without the prior written consent of the publisher.

Originally published by International Youth Mission
Calle 22c # 31 - 01
Santafe de Bogotá D.C.
Colombia

Design and diagrams by: Camila Díaz Torres‾
Illustrations by: Camila Díaz Torres
Revised by: Luisa Del Río Saavedra

Copyright for this version © 2001 by Dovewell Publications

Translated and produced by Dovewell Communications

All scriptural quotations are from the New King James Version, Thomas Nelson Inc., 1991

Original title: Consolidación: Proceso eficaz para formar discípulos

Translated and produced by Dovewell Publications
Kensington Temple, Kensington Park Road
London W11 3BY England

Printed in Belarus by World Wide Printing

ISBN 1-898-444-06-4

Printcorp. LP № 347 of 11.05.99. Kuprevich St. 18, Minsk. 220141. Or. 01101. Qty 10 000 cps.

CONTENTS

ACKNOWLEDGEMENTS

I am thankful to the many people whose constant efforts, support, testimonies and prayers made this book possible.

Firstly, I want to thank God for giving me the opportunity to serve in His work. I want to thank Him also for giving me a church with a vision — International Charismatic Mission (MCI) — as well as pastors who believed in my husband and me. I also want to thank Pastors César and Claudia Castellanos for giving me the opportunity to do new things for the Lord, and for giving me fresh challenges. They inspired me by their own faith and testimony to trust in a big God, a God capable of changing lives, of transforming nations and of turning the impossible into reality.

In addition, I want to thank the Youth of MCI for believing in us, the pastors. And I'd like to thank all the leaders in our church who understand the meaning of 'consolidation' and are giving their best to keep every soul that God has placed into our hands.

Thank you to my beloved husband who sacrificed his time to bring this book to fruition. César, thank you for your love, your advice, your patience, your valuable suggestions and your unconditional support. I will always be thankful to God for uniting us. You are the best gift God has given me. Together we will do great things for the Lord and we will lift up his name across the nations.

Thank you also to my sweet children, Josué and Alejandro, my dynamic duo, for giving me their time, their love and also for waiting for me when I needed them to wait. I love both of you very much and I know you will reap everything you have sown.

Finally, thank you Holy Spirit, for being my source of inspiration, and for giving me the thoughts and strategies to accomplish the work which you have placed in my heart to do. Thank you for believing in me and for being the sweetest and most affectionate person I have ever known. I love you Holy Spirit, and my greatest desire is to please you and to fulfil your perfect will.

INTRODUCTION

We are living in a time of revival. God is touching the hearts of men and women so that they will know His will for their lives. With this awakening the church faces a real challenge: to fulfil the Great Commission given in Matthew 28: 19-20, "Go, therefore, and make disciples of all the nations..."

One of the great difficulties we have in the church at the moment is to retain every soul that makes a commitment to Christ. The commandment given to the church is to make disciples not decisions. This is not just a job to be done on one day, but a lifestyle.

We, as the church of Jesus Christ, have to accept the responsibility and seriousness that this privilege demands, and must look deeper into consolidation to find out what it is and what it requires of us.

We have to love consolidation and be prepared to do the work to make it a reality. For this reason, you should get to know this material.

Study each topic in detail before moving on, as each chapter goes deeper into the subject. This way, you will learn how to present the material and be able to use it with new believers.

In every chapter you will find a revision exercise for your personal study. These will help you to achieve excellent results in your ministry.

I am sure that after studying this book you will not only be a little more knowledgeable, but you will make consolidation part of your life. It will become a habit to consolidate all who give their lives to Jesus in celebrations, Sunday services, and also in your cell meetings.

In the first chapter, you will learn what consolidation is, the importance that it has in the heart of God, its purpose, and what it requires of the consolidator.

In the second chapter, the importance of prayer for the success of consolidation is explained, together with some models of intercession.

In the third, we look at the moment when the person makes their decision for Christ, the five lessons on evangelism and the verification of the decision. In the fourth the allocation, and in the fifth the initial phone call and the pastoral care given by phone.

In the sixth chapter, you will find a guide to ministering to the new believer during your visit. Lastly, we will look at the questions most commonly raised by new believers. Also I have prepared some short sermons which can be used for preaching to the new believer.

It is my desire that, as you put this teaching into practice, you will also see growth in your church.

May the Lord support you as He did the early church, adding every day to your cell, ministry or church, those who are being saved.

"And the Lord added to the church daily those who were being saved."

Acts 2:47

FOREWORD

In the seminars that I have given throughout the world, I have observed that pastors everywhere want to know how to close the back door of the church, the door through which many new believers leave and never return. One of the biggest difficulties we face in all evangelistic campaigns is to retain the fruit.

This problem becomes a vicious circle for many churches. While you are out searching for new believers, others are being lost through the back door. To all such pastors, I present a key that will successfully lock the church's back door. This key is called consolidation.

This book that you have in your hand is not just a book. It is one of the secrets of solid and sustainable growth. I believe that the work of evangelists is very important and the blame for the low percentage of people who remain in the church does not lie with them.

They have done their bit by bringing fruit into the churches. Consolidation generates commitment and faithfulness, because everyone has a role to play.

It is clear that some pastors have not been properly trained in how to build and mature new believers. Every pastor has a deep desire to see their church grow, and they become frustrated when people from their congregations leave and go to another church. They get upset with other pastors instead of asking themselves what they are doing wrong.

Consolidation is like a watch where every part is equally important. In this book you will doubtless find teaching that appears to be very simple, and which you might even wish to ignore. I want to say, however, that in a watch there are parts that are very simple but without which the watch would cease to work. In the same way, every topic in this book is essential for success in the process of consolidation.

Consolidation is the answer to the pastoral needs of today. If you are reading this book in preparation for starting a ministry, or if you are a believer who wants to see solid and sustainable growth in your church, I suggest you take a copy of this book to your pastor, as it will encourage him to introduce the consolidation process to his church.

I am sure that the teaching in this book will help you to increase your own vision concerning the growth of your church. And pastors will discover untapped potential in every believer, and will find out how to involve them in this ministry.

I congratulate Claudia Fajardo for all her efforts in making this book, "Consolidation: an effective process for making disciples", a reality. Behind each page are sleepless nights, tears, fasting and many prayers. Thanks to her perseverance, this book has not only blessed our church but will also bless other nations.

César Castellanos
Senior Pastor,
International Charismatic Mission

CONSOLIDATION

CONSOLIDATION

AN EFFECTIVE PROCESS
FOR MAKING DISCIPLES

One of the last things that Jesus said before He left the earth was that He wanted us to make disciples of all nations. Every believer needs to understand what it means to be a disciple of Jesus and what their responsibility is in relation to the Great Commission.

This involves everyone in the church of Jesus Christ, irrespective of race or social status. The church is the only instrument God has to bring about Jesus' dream of taking His Word to all the earth.

When Jesus spoke of making disciples, He was thinking of two aspects: the going and the making.

The going is essentially what the church does for those who don't yet know Jesus, for those who have not yet heard the message of salvation through the cross and have therefore not been able to make a decision for or against following Jesus.

The going is therefore the church's first step in seeking to carry out Jesus' commandment, but it's not the only one. The call to make disciples goes much further. It's more than just preaching the gospel. Discipleship is all about shaping people, about nurturing the spiritually new born baby. It is about reaffirming the new believer's decision for Christ in such a way that they experience a genuine change in their lifestyle and become involved in the life of the church. They need to be taught how to begin their new lifestyle, as well as how to change to become effective witnesses for Jesus.

"Go therefore and make disciples of all the nations..."

Matthew 28:19

"Teaching them to observe all things that I have commanded you; and lo, I am with you always, even to the end of the age."

Matthew 28:20

What Is Consolidation?

Consolidation can be defined as 'the care and attention we should give to the new believer in order to reproduce Christ's character in him or her'. By doing this we ensure that they will fulfil God's purpose for their lives and bear fruit that will last (John 15:16).

This fruit must be sufficiently evident in their changed lives to be able to reproduce fruit in others.

The Apostle Paul provides us with a great example of what it means to look after souls. He achieved great things for God and developed a great ministry. The secret of his success was to care for people properly and to value them in the same way that God values them. You too can be as effective as Paul, but remember, he gave everything for his disciples.

OBJECTIVES OF CONSOLIDATION

- To look after every new believer, aware of their value to God, and ensure they bear lasting fruit for the Lord.
- To reproduce in them the character of Jesus.
- To keep in the church every new believer that God has placed in our hands.
- To turn every believer into a disciple maker.

We have to care for people properly and to value them in the same way that God values them.

A good example of the work and effort required is found in Colossians 1:28 – 29

"Him we preach, warning every man and teaching every man in all wisdom, that we may present every man perfect in Christ Jesus. To this end I also labour, striving according to His working which works in me mightily."

In this scripture "striving" means to make every effort. The kind of "labour" needed will be demanding and exhausting.

Consolidation demands exhaustive work…

We need to work diligently at consolidation. But when we are motivated by love and a deep desire to fulfil God's desire for us, to love and care for souls, we will experience great satisfaction.

REVISION

CONSOLIDATION: AN EFFECTIVE PROCESS

OBJECTIVE

To demonstrate how consolidation is an effective process which produces excellent results.

We can see how Jesus took care of and shepherded His disciples and confirmed His love and acceptance of them from the very moment He called them until He left them as strong and solid pillars of His church.

Answer the following questions:

1. THE CALL

According to **Mark 1:16 – 19**

1.1 What job were Andrew and Simon doing?

_____

_____

_____

1.2 Who approaches them near to Lake Galilee?

_____

_____

1.3 Who is looking for whom?

_____

_____

_____

This implies that Jesus moved away from His comfort zone and went to the place where He needed to go in order to find those He was calling.

1.4 To what did He call them?

_____

_____

1.5 Who were they going to remain with?

_____

_____

2. THE PRAYER

In His priestly ministry, Jesus knew the privilege and the responsibility of coming before God in prayer for His team and also for the new believers reached by them.

Read **John 17:20** and answer the following questions:

2.1 For whom did Jesus pray?

_____

_____

2.2 Through what means would they come to faith?

_____

_____

2.3 According to **John 17:15** what did Jesus ask His Father for regarding His disciples?

_____

_____

_____

3. THE VISIT

In **Mark 1:29 – 31** we find Jesus spending time with Peter:

3.1 Where exactly are they?

_____

_____

3.2 What did He do there?

_____

Peter and his family were greatly influenced by what Jesus did because He met a need and showed a personal interest in them.

4. THE TEACHING

Throughout the four Gospels we see that Jesus constantly taught His disciples. These were not just theoretical lessons, but He also spent time with them demonstrating how they should live the new lifestyle.

4.1 According to **Matthew 13:10 –12** why do you believe that Jesus considered it vitally important to explain things properly to His disciples and to make an effort to ensure they understood what He was teaching?

_____

_____

_____

5. THE SENDING OUT
How do we know that Jesus' three years, spent intensively training His disciples were effective? The answer is that Jesus proved it when He sent them out to do exactly what they had seen Him doing in His ministry.

According to **Mark 6:7–13:**

5.1 How did He send them out?

_____

5.2 What were they to take with them?

_____
_____

5.3 What were they to preach?

_____
_____
_____
_____

5.4 How do you think Jesus supported them in this task?

_____
_____
_____
_____
_____
_____
_____
_____

We can conclude from these scriptures that Jesus Christ gave us the best example of how to consolidate people. His results are clear to all and have implications for us today.

"In the morning sow your seed, and in the evening do not withhold your hand; for you do not know which will prosper, either this or that, or whether both alike will be good."

Ecclesiastes 11:6

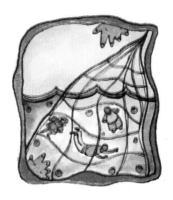

"And I will make you fishers of men"
Matthew 4:19

PRINCIPLES OF CONSOLIDATION

When Jesus called His first disciples He told them that He would make them fishers of men.

One of the most common methods of fishing on the Sea of Galilee is for two boats to work in harmony. A fisherman on each boat holds one side of the net each and they drag the net in between the two boats. The net has weights to make it sink and also ropes to hold on to. When the catch is a heavy one, one of the fishermen will turn his boat and come alongside his partner.

They work together pulling the ropes and throwing stones at the fish to scare them into staying in the net. When they get close to the beach they row the boats ashore pulling the full net behind them. Once on the beach, the fish are sorted according to the different types.

This method of fishing shows us the real value of team effort. Some row while others pull the net with great force. At the same time others throw stones so the fish are scared and do not escape from the net. This is a great example of teamwork. Each one does his own task in a corporate effort!

Retaining souls is not only the pastor's work, but it's the job of everyone in the church. Success does not depend only on one person, but on the entire team.

Success does not depend only on one person, but on the whole team.

Let's look now at some passages of Scripture to discover the biblical principles of consolidation, which produced excellent results in the time of the apostles.

Acts 2 records the first sermon Peter gave to 3,000 people who then responded to the gospel, and the steps taken by the apostles to retain this fruit. A close look at this passage will help us with the consolidation process and to achieve the same results in our time.

1 VERIFYING SALVATION

According to **Acts 2:41**, those who heard the Word were baptised. It was normal at that time for the genuineness of salvation to be tested through their repentance and the confession of their sins and through their willingness to be baptised in water.

2 TEACHING DOCTRINE TO THE NEW BELIEVER

In **Acts 2:42** we see how the apostles persevered in teaching them doctrine. *Every day* they joined together in the temple and were *continually* and *consistently* teaching the doctrine of Jesus.

Because of this, the Scripture says that they became such an influence that they enjoyed the favour of people around. This demonstrates how they lived out in their lives everything they had learnt.

3 FELLOWSHIP

(Acts 2:46 – 47)

Verse 42 says:
"...they continued steadfastly in the apostles' doctrine and fellowship...". By nature people are social beings and we need one another to grow and develop. We are called to create the right atmosphere in which new believers will find a sense of belonging to the family of God.

4 HOLINESS

"...they continued steadfastly ... in the breaking of bread" Acts 2:42

"For he who eats and drinks in an unworthy manner eats and drinks judgement to himself, not discerning the Lord's body."
1 Corinthians 11:29

The most important requirement for participation in the Lord's Supper is holiness. When the apostles administered the Lord's Supper they emphasised the need for all believers to keep themselves free from sin so they would not face judgement or death. This should be taught to new believers to encourage them to live in holiness.

5 PRAYER

"...they continued steadfastly ... in prayers".
Acts 2:42

The disciples were people of prayer and it goes without saying that they would teach new believers to pray constantly. We should understand how prayer moves the hand of God, releases His power and gives us the anointing necessary to see results.

1. Verifying salvation
This must be done in a way that causes the new believer to reaffirm his decision and to overcome any preconceived ideas that they may have.

2. Doctrine
To teach the new believers a new lifestyle.

3. Fellowship
To promote Christian fellowship in the family of God.

4. Holiness
Consecration through participation in the Lord's supper.

5. Prayer
- Releases God's power
- Gives God's anointing
- Produces results

By doing these things we will find that, just as in the times of the apostles: **the Lord will add every day those who are being saved.**

In summary: those principles applied by the early church to consolidate new believers are:

1 Verifying salvation
2 Teaching doctrine to new believers
3 Fellowship
4 Holiness
5 Prayer

The question is, can these principles work today? The answer can be found in Acts 2:47 "And the Lord added to the church daily those who were being saved". This demonstrates that there was continuous growth. If we apply the same principles, we will surely have exactly the same results as those obtained by the early church, and the Lord will add every day to the church those who are going to be saved.

REVISION

PRINCIPLES OF CONSOLIDATION

OBJECTIVE
To apply the principles used by the early church to new believers.

1. **VERIFICATION OF SALVATION**
   In order for the new believer to remain with the Lord and persevere in the Christian life, they should take their decision for Christ seriously.

1.1 According to **Acts 2:38**
What was necessary to know forgiveness of sins?

_____

_____

_____

1.2 How are you able to create in people an awareness of the necessity of receiving forgiveness of sins?

_____

_____

_____

_____

2. **TEACHING DOCTRINE TO NEW BELIEVERS**
   The formation of Christ's character in all new converts requires consistency and perseverance.

2.1 According to **Acts 2:46** what did the new believers persevere in?

_____

_____

_____

2.2 Read **Hebrews 13:17** and explain the reasons
why we should attend church meetings.

_____

_____

_____

_____

2.3 Based on your own personal experience, how would
you teach new believers about the importance and
benefits of attending a church or cell group?

_____

_____

_____

_____

_____

3. FELLOWSHIP
The apostles were very aware of reaching new
believers with friendship, as well as promoting unity
and harmony amongst all believers, irrespective of how
long they had been believers.

3.1 From **Acts 2:44** complete the sentence below.

_____who believed were
_____and had all things in common

3.2 What is the meaning of **Proverbs 18:24** and what
relevance do you think it has for the process
of consolidation?

_____

_____

_____

_____

3.3 In **Acts 2:46**, in which place do the new believers gather together to share?

_____

_____

_____

4. HOLINESS

The early church emphasised holiness and invited only those who were clean before God to participate in the Lord's Supper. One of the results of holiness was that outsiders would see their purity.

4.1 Read **Acts 2:46–47** and explain what "and having favour with all the people" means.

_____

_____

_____

_____

4.2 Read **1 Timothy 3:7** How should a believer behave towards outsiders, and why?

_____

_____

4.3 Do you think there is any connection between having favour with the people and having a good testimony?

_____

Why?_____

_____

_____

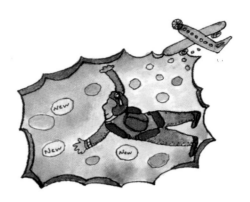

GETTING READY
TO CONSOLIDATE

If you were a paratrooper going on an aeroplane and knew in advance that you would need a parachute, you would certainly prepare carefully, taking care of every detail so that you would not take any unnecessary risks with your life.

In the same way, all of us who want to be successful consolidators should prepare ourselves to the highest standards of excellence. It is necessary to be totally committed, and when you do your part God will not leave you ashamed. He will do even greater things than all you could ask or desire (Ephesians 3:20).

Preparation is founded upon the following:

1 HOLINESS

Whoever aspires to be used by God needs to be holy. God only uses instruments that are clean so that He can flow through them to do His work. God does not mix the holy with the profane, which is why He never pours out His presence and His anointing into an unclean vessel.

Holiness is not just something that we should desire; it's also the way to see God's presence rest upon our lives.

Hosea 10:12
"Sow for yourselves righteousness; reap in mercy; break up your fallow ground, for it is time to seek the Lord, til He comes and rains righteousness on you."

The unploughed ground referred to is the ground that has become hard through lack of use between harvests. It has hardened itself and needs to be softened and broken up so that it can again receive new seed.

Finally, remember the only thing that takes away God's authority and support from your life is secret, unconfessed sin. If that is true in your life, do not justify yourself or blame others, rather go before God and put it right.

2 COMPASSION

Love was the key to success for Jesus. He demonstrated this when He left His throne of glory to be like us, denying Himself, going to where the needy people were, sharing their affliction and problems and identifying with them. His priority was meeting the needs of those who came to Him.

3 KNOWING THE WORD

All the people God has used throughout history gave priority in their lives to the Word of God. You will find in the Word of God the foundation of all wisdom and spiritual growth.

We need to remain completely dependent on the Word of God. Only through the Word can we give answers to those who are searching for help and advice. The great preacher, Spurgeon read through the Bible more than 100 times. He said: *'The last time I read it I found it much more beautiful than the first time'.*

Always remember that you should only answer the questions of new believers from the Word of God (Matthew 4:4).

4 THE RIGHT ATTITUDE

Send me!!

Colossians 3:23
"And whatever you do, do it heartily, as to the Lord and not to men".

One of the things that pleases God the most is when we do our work for Him, and not for those around us. We should work as if God were doing it Himself, and we should do it with fervour, excellence and passion, as if our own life depended upon it.

Our attitude should be determined by spending time listening to His voice and being sensitive to His direction. We are not to lay hands on others rashly, or minister deliverance impulsively, as this will only cause fear and confusion in the new believer.

5 PRAYER

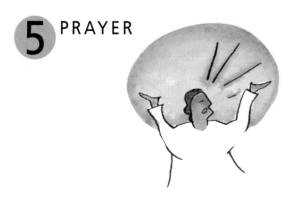

If there is one thing that we should become specialists in, it is prayer. Every battle that we desire to win in the earthly realm, must first be won in the heavenlies.

Let us make prayer the most special time of the day. Avoid making it boring, mechanical and monotonous. If it becomes like that, it will be lukewarm prayer and there will be no breakthrough because we are not speaking from the heart.

Remember that we are talking to the Lord Himself, the wisest person in the universe. Think about what you are saying to Him, but speak simply and be to the point. Hold on to John 6:37 "…and the one who comes to Me I will by no means cast out". Be confident and honest with the Lord, because He is there to hear you.

1. HOLINESS

"Break up your unploughed ground". Holiness is a fundamental requirement of being used by God.
The only thing that takes away God's authority and support is unconfessed sin in your life.

2. COMPASSION

Love was the key in Jesus' ministry.

3. KNOWING THE WORD

Müller discovered the widespread error of reading much about the Bible but reading hardly anything of the Bible. The Word became the source of his inspiration and the secret of his marvellous spiritual growth.

4. ATTITUDE

"Also I heard the voice of the Lord saying:

'Whom shall I send, and who will go for Us?' Then I said, Here am I!, Send me"

Isaiah 6:8

5. PRAYER

Prayer breaks all chains!
"Call to Me, and I will answer you, and show you great and mighty things, which you do not know"
Jeremiah 33:3

We must first conquer in the spiritual realm everything that we desire to conquer in the earthly realm.

 **REVISION**

GETTING READY TO CONSOLIDATE

OBJECTIVE
To demonstrate that all men and women used by God throughout Bible history, and the history of humanity, displayed the same characteristics in their lives.

1. HOLINESS

Samuel was consecrated to God in his early years, and the result was that he grew in holiness. According to **1 Samuel 2** what are the results of growth?

1.1 1 Samuel 2:26

_____
_____
_____
_____

1.2 1 Samuel 3:19

_____
_____
_____
_____

1.3 1 Samuel 3:20

_____
_____
_____
_____

This continuous growth is manifested primarily in holiness in the life of Samuel. This holiness gave him the privilege of bringing down the presence of God not only at Shiloh, but also throughout Israel.

2. COMPASSION

The word 'compassion' in the original Greek is *splanchnon* meaning inward parts. It is from here that strong emotions originate, such as tender mercy, feelings of affection, compassion, sympathy and godliness.

How do we know that the Apostle Paul had compassion?

2.1 Galatians 4:12

_____

_____

_____

_____

2.2 Galatians 4:19

_____

_____

_____

_____

2.3 Philippians 1:8

_____

_____

_____

_____

2.4 Moved by this compassion, what did Paul do?
Romans 15:19,20.

_____

_____

_____

_____

_____

3. KNOWLEDGE

3.1 What evidence did Peter give that he had extensive
knowledge of the Scriptures? **Acts 2:14–35**

_____

_____

_____

_____

3.2 What did this knowledge of the Scriptures produce
in those who listened? **Acts 2:37**

_____

_____

_____

_____

4. RIGHT ATTITUDE

4.1 According to **Jonah 1:1–3** what was Jonah's reaction
the first time God asked him to take His Word
to Nineveh?

_____

_____

_____

_____

4.2 Look at **Jonah 3:1–3** and write down what Jonah did when the Lord gave him a second chance to preach.

_____

_____

_____

_____

_____

4.3 What were the consequences for Nineveh of Jonah's attitude? **Jonah 3:4–10**

_____

_____

_____

_____

_____

5. PRAYER

5.1 Jesus is the greatest example to us of how necessary it is to pray in order to get results. In **Mark 1:35** what did Jesus do before preaching?

_____

_____

5.2 What motivated Jesus to spend time in prayer? **Mark 1:38–39**

_____

_____

_____

**"Then I will raise up for Myself a faithful Priest who shall do according to what is in My heart and in My mind. I will build him a sure house, and he shall walk before My anointed forever"
1 Samuel 2:35.**

PRAYER
THAT OVERCOMES

PRAYER
THAT OVERCOMES

The most powerful weapon given by God to Christians is prayer. We have to pray intelligently in order to get results.

Daniel Chapter 9 is a good biblical example of what can be done in the life of a man and in his nation through prayer. We will see how by the application of four basic principles:

1 Taking a personal interest in the people

Daniel 9:3
"Then I set my face toward to the Lord God to make request by prayer and supplications, with fasting, sackcloth and ashes".

2 Confessing the sins of the people as though they are your own

Daniel 9:5
"We have sinned and committed iniquity, we have done wickedly and rebelled, even by departing from Your precepts and Your judgements".

3 Seeking God's mercy

Daniel 9:18
"O my God, incline your ear and hear; open your eyes and see our desolations, and the city which is called by your name; for we do not present our supplications before You because of our righteous deeds, but because of Your great mercies".

Promoting perseverance in prayer –

4. Promoting perseverance in prayer – a battle in the spiritual realm

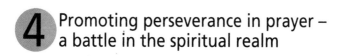

Daniel 10:13
"But the prince of the kingdom of Persia
withstood me twenty–one days..."

With these principles in mind, we should adopt the
following method for our own prayer:

---

1. Personal Interest
Take an interest in and look at the situation of those
you are planning to reach. What things are blinding,
enslaving or destroying them?

2. Confess the sins of the people as if they are your own
Confess your own sins, those of other people
and those of your Government.

3. Plead for Mercy
Claim appropriate biblical promises. For example,
2 Corinthians 10:5 and **John 16:8**.

4. Declare War in the Spiritual Realm
"So I sought for a man among them who would make a wall,
and stand in the gap before Me on behalf of the land, that I
should not destroy it; but I found no one."
Ezekiel 22:30

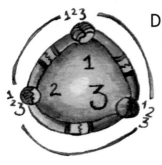

DAILY COMMITMENT TO INTERCESSORY PRAYER

Weekly intercessions
with the team

PRAYING IN THREES

In intercessory prayer, you are presenting yourself before God on behalf of other people. You should rise up in intercessory prayer each day before God. As you pray privately, or in groups of three, you will be small groups co–operating and in unity with the overall plan and purpose of the church. The key here is to pray for people whom God is going to save and bring through the consolidation process for us to look after and edify. In interceding we can apply the principles we have learnt from the book of Daniel.

PRAYER OF THREE

DATE BEGUN

PLACE AND TIME OF PRAYER IN UNITY

DATE OF FIRST CONTACT

DATE AND LOCATION OF SECOND CONTACT

DATES OF INVITATION TO THE CHURCH

PRAYER OF THREE

NAME OF THE THREE PRAYER WARRIORS:

1.

2.

3.

FUTURE CHRISTIANS BEING PRAYED FOR:

1.

2.

3.

1.

2.

3.

1.

2.

3.

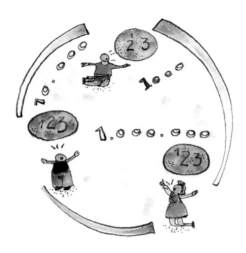

REMEMBER:
With the prayers of one, a thousand flee. With the prayers of two, ten thousand flee! How many will flee with the prayers of three?

COVENANT PRAYER OF THREE

Agree to pray in your threesome for nine people for a whole month - on your own every day, and once a week as a group of three.

"How could one chase a thousand, and two put ten thousand to flight, unless their Rock had sold them, and the Lord had surrendered them?"

Deuteronomy 32:30

 **REVISION**

PRAYER THAT OVERCOMES

When we become aware of the war that exists between the kingdom of darkness and the Kingdom of God, we ought to become actively involved in this warfare – all the more so when we realise we have the victory.

1. HAVING A PERSONAL INTEREST IN THE PEOPLE

Read **Daniel 11 – 13** and answer the following questions:

1.1 How did Daniel seek the Lord? (v13)

_____
_____
_____
_____

1.2 What was the situation of Jerusalem at that time?

_____
_____
_____
_____

1.3 Why did Daniel want to see the restoration of Jerusalem?

_____
_____
_____
_____

2. CONFESS THE SINS OF THE PEOPLE AS IF THEY WERE YOUR OWN

According to **Daniel 9:5–15**:

2.1 What did Daniel do in his prayer? (v5–6)

_____
_____
_____

2.2 Do you believe that Daniel participated in those sins he confessed? Give reasons for your answer.

_____
_____

When we confess other people's sins as if they are our own, this shows compassion and motivates us to become part of the solution.

3. PLEAD FOR MERCY

Read **Daniel 9: 16-19**
There is none righteous, not even one. The right attitude to get closer to God is through His mercy.

3.1 Was the punishment of those that were suffering justified?

_____
_____
_____

3.2 According to verse 18 what did Daniel put his trust in when he sought the Lord?

_____
_____

4. PERSIST IN SPIRITUAL WARFARE AND PRAYER.

In the light of **Daniel 10:12–13** answer the following questions:

4.1 At what moment did the Lord hear and answer Daniel's prayer?

_____
_____
_____
_____

4.2 What happened when the answer was sent?

_____
_____

4.3 Who came to help Gabriel?

_____
_____

4.4 What do you think happened between Gabriel, Michael and the Prince of the kingdom of Persia?

_____
_____
_____
_____

What caused the breakthrough? When we pray to God with the right attitude He sends His response immediately. If the enemy rises up in opposition then through prayer we wage war in the spiritual realm.

Winning things in the spiritual realm brings answers in the physical world.

VERIFICATION

VERIFICATION

In practice, the verification process starts as soon as the preaching is over, and everyone bows their heads. The prayer of salvation is prayed, and an invitation is given to those who prayed that prayer for the first time to stand up and come to the front.

Once the new believers have moved into the consolidation room, the consolidator must explain very clearly the work of Christ. He or she will use the five lessons on evangelism (see below). The intention is that the new believers should understand exactly what they are doing. Matthew 13:19 teaches how the enemy stole the word that had been sown when the people did not understand it.

5 FIVE LESSONS ON EVANGELISM

1 The teaching of love

2 The teaching about sin

3 The teaching of Christ as the only and sufficient Saviour

4 The teaching on repentance

5 The teaching about accepting Christ

1 THE TEACHING ABOUT LOVE

In order to explain this teaching clearly, we need to use biblical passages that teach about God's love for every individual. We need to take hold of the passages such as

Jeremiah 31:3
"…I have loved you with an everlasting love; therefore with lovingkindness I have drawn you."

You should also use John 16:27 and John 10:10.

2 THE TEACHING ABOUT SIN

Use verses that show that everyone, without exception, has sinned, for example, Romans 3:23 and Romans 3:10–12.

Emphasise that although God has a profound love for His creation, people have forgotten about Him and have become wise in their own opinion and do evil in His sight.

Romans 3:12
"They have all turned aside; they have together become unprofitable; there is none who does good, no, not one".

3 THE TEACHING OF CHRIST AS THE ONLY SUFFICIENT SAVIOUR

John 14:16; Galatians 3:13;
Ephesians 2:8,9; Isaiah 53:5;
1 John 1:7.
The objective of our evangelism
should always be to present Christ
crucified for our sins. No message of
evangelism would be complete
without mentioning this supreme act
of redemption.

Romans 5:8
"But God demonstrates His own love
toward us, in that while we were still
sinners, Christ died for us."

4 THE TEACHING ON REPENTANCE

Acts 3:19;
1 John 1:9; Isaiah 1:18;
Proverbs 28:13

You should emphasise to the
new believer that if he asks
God with all his heart to
wipe away his past life, God

will do it. Tell the new believer that God looks at the heart, and He looks for genuine repentance.

As Acts 3:19 shows, repentance changes your way of thinking and enables you to adjust your ideas to the parameters laid down by God. The new believer should be aware that changing your way of thinking changes your goals, your attitudes and the way you live your life (Romans 12:1-2).

5 THE TEACHING ON ACCEPTING OR RECEIVING CHRIST

Matthew 7:13–14
John 1:12
This is the climax! We have to be inventive in our approach. Explain that only the courageous are able to accept the challenge, by opening their hearts to Christ. Motivate them to do this. Tell them that this is the moment to say:
'Lord, I recognise the wrong way I have been living my life, and how much I need you. Come and guide me from here onwards. Be enthroned in my heart.'

Revelation 3:20
"Behold, I stand at the door and knock.
If anyone hears My voice and opens the
door, I come in to him and dine with
him, and he with Me."

You may also use the passages in
Romans 10:9-10; Matthew 7:13–14,
and John 1:12.

Do not forget to keep an open heart and to act
according to the guidance of the Holy Spirit. Lastly,
pray the prayer of faith, but be sure that the person
praying recognises and acknowledges their sin, asks
for forgiveness and, by faith, accepts Jesus as their
Lord and Saviour.

**IN THE PRAYER OF REPENTANCE,
EMPHASISE FOUR THINGS:**

1 Their need of God: "I need you"

2 Their condition: "I am a sinner"

3 Their repentance: "Forgive me,
I don't want to fail you"

4 Their acceptance: "I receive you!
I believe in you!"

MODEL PRAYER

> Dear Lord Jesus, I believe in you. I realise that I need your forgiveness and your love. Come and cleanse my life from all my sin, as I do not want to fail you any more. Guide my steps from this day onwards. Today, I receive you as my Lord and only sufficient Saviour, so that I can enjoy the abundant life that you won for me on the Cross.

When they have made their decision and prayed the prayer, check that it is genuine.

FIVE LESSONS ON EVANGELISM

1. The teaching of love
John 3:16; Jeremiah 31:3; John 10:10

2. Teaching about sin
Romans 3:23; Romans 3:10-12

3. Teaching about Christ as the only sufficient Saviour
John 14:6; Galatians 3:13;
Ephesians 2:8,9; Isaiah 53:5; 1 John 1:7

4. Teaching about Repentance
Acts 3:19; 1 John 1:9; Isaiah 1:18;
Proverbs 28:13

5. Teaching on Acceptance or Receiving Christ
Revelation 3:20;
Matthew 7:13-14; John 1:12

VERIFYING THEIR SALVATION

OBJECTIVE

1 To show and confirm the love of God for everyone.

2 To make sure they have received Jesus and understood that He is now in their heart.

3 To find out their needs and show them that Christ can supply all those needs.

It is now time to confirm and establish the new believer's salvation.

1 INTRODUCE YOURSELF

Be spontaneous and try to win their confidence. Be friendly, smile at them and ask for their name! Make sure you memorise it! Win their trust! These steps will make them feel important!

2 BREAK THE ICE

Remember that you are in control of the situation and that you have the initiative. Ask simple questions, for example: How did you find the meeting? How did you feel?

3 ASK SIMPLE DIAGNOSTIC QUESTIONS

According to the guidance of the leader,
ask the following questions:

> **Q.** Where is Christ now?
> **A.** In my heart.
>
> **Q.** Why do you think He is there?
> **A.** Because the Word of God says so,
> and I believe it!
>
> **Q.** What did Christ do on the Cross?
> **A.** He died for my sins.
>
> **Q.** What do you have to do to be saved?
> **A.** Believe in Christ and accept Him into my heart.

4 INTRODUCE OR REINFORCE SPECIFIC TEACHING POINTS THAT ARE RELEVANT TO THE PERSON YOU ARE CONSOLIDATING

If they feel they are good and do not feel they need to
repent, reinforce the teaching on sin.

If they feel they cannot be forgiven for their sins,
reinforce the teaching on Christ as the only and
sufficient Saviour.

5 FILL OUT THE VERIFICATION FORM

If possible, give them some refreshments and fill out the form with them. This will save time in subsequent days because the information recorded will be accurate. Do not forget to make a note of their needs, as this will open the door for future telephone calls and visits.

6 PRAY FOR THEM

Get them to hold hands with you and pray for their needs, for their blessing and protection, and seal them in the body of Christ, which is the church.

Finally, ask them if they would like to receive more direction or counselling. If so, get the appropriate person to contact them if you are unable to do this.

SUMMARY OF VERIFICATION

1 INTRODUCE YOURSELF

2 BREAK THE ICE

3 ASK SIMPLE DIAGNOSTIC QUESTIONS

4 INTRODUCE OR REINFORCE
THE MOST RELEVANT TEACHING

5 FILL OUT THE VERIFICATION FORM

6 PRAY FOR THEM

ALLOCATION

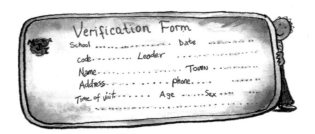

ALLOCATION

Once the verification forms have been collected in, they are distributed to the team assigned to do the follow–up work.

The new believer will be allocated to the cell group nearest to where he or she lives. Sometimes a person may live in a neighbourhood where there is no cell group. This will provide a good opportunity to open a new one. In this way, the entire city will be filled with the gospel.

It is important that you choose people with the right skills and character for this crucial job. They need to be present–day Samaritans, people capable of winning the city for the Lord. We know that every soul is valuable, so the follow–up work should only be allocated to leaders who are able to give of their very best, ensuring that no souls are lost.

Remember to use the verification forms, and do not put off the phone call for too long. Every verification form that comes into your hands represents a soul bought at a very high price, indeed at an invaluable price: the blood of Jesus.

We see in Acts 9:10–11 just how valuable Paul's soul was to God. We see Christ's desire for him to be visited. He gave Ananias the exact address — Judas' house in Straight Street, Damascus City. Seeing how special souls are to the Lord, there can be no doubt that He also keeps a record of the person to whom He entrusted each new believer.

Give yourself a challenge – to give your best to the Lord. Do everything you are capable of doing in order to reach the people who have been entrusted to you, and be confident that you *will* reap if you do not lose heart.

"Deliver those who are drawn toward death, and hold back those stumbling to the slaughter. If you say, ' Surely we did not know this,' does not He who weighs the hearts consider it? He who keeps your soul, does He not know it? And will He not render to each man according to his deeds?"

Proverbs 24:11–12

Someone once said:
If not now, when?
If not here, where?
If not me, who?

THE PHONE CALL

THE PHONE CALL

The phone call is, in effect, a visit by phone. It is a key to successful evangelism, and should be undertaken with excellence and for the benefit of the new believer, to consolidate them and confirm their salvation. The telephone is a medium which helps us to communicate, and we should use today's technology to spread the Kingdom of God. In the time of the apostle Paul, letters were used. Either way, the goal is to discover the spiritual condition or personal circumstances of the new believer in order to help with counselling or exhortation.

PURPOSE OF THE PHONE CALL

1 To show a genuine interest in the person and in their need.

2 To win the confidence of the new believer.

3 To leave a way open for a follow-up visit.

PREPARING TO MAKE THE CALL

1 In prayer.

Work out an appropriate place for the visit . **2**

3 Planning the time.

HOW TO MAKE THE CALL

1 **Say Hello**
This has to be done in a friendly way. When you talk to the new believer, identify yourself as a member of the church to which you belong.

2 **Start the conversation**
You should begin the conversation naturally and with warmth, telling them that you have prayed for their need and that you would like to know how they are doing.

3 **Assess their spiritual condition**
Ask them how they found the meeting and how they feel about their relationship with God since visiting the church.

4 **Confirm the home visit**
Make a firm appointment, place, date and time. Give them various alternatives: their home, a cafe, but never at the church.

5 **Pray for them**
Always finish by praying for them according to the leading of the Holy Spirit.

STRATEGIES FOR SUCCESS

1 Always be pleasant and friendly

2 Avoid:

- Being harsh or impatient during the conversation.

- Putting pressure on the new believer.

- Taking more time than necessary.

- Arguing or confronting.

- Showing self–interest, rather than considering the needs of the other person.

REMEMBER THE OBJECTIVES:

To show genuine interest in the person
and in their needs.

To win their confidence.

To leave the way open to make a home visit

"Surely you shall call a nation you do not know, and
nations who do not know you shall run to you, because
of the Lord your God, and the Holy One of Israel; for He
has glorified you."

Isaiah 55:5

REVISION

SALVATION, ALLOCATION
AND PHONE CALL

The Word says in **2 Corinthians 6:2,** *"For He says, 'In an acceptable time I have heard you, and in the day of salvation I have helped you'".*

When we embark on the process of consolidation, we should look for the appropriate time and date to do it, then we shall do it with excellence.

Answer the following questions from what you have learnt:

1. What are the objectives in the verification of the new believer?

_____
_____
_____
_____
_____

2. What are the five lessons on evangelism? Give a Bible verse for each one.

_____
_____
_____
_____
_____
_____
_____
_____
_____
_____

3. Regarding the five lessons on Evangelism:

3.1 What would you say to a person who does not feel important to God?

_____
_____
_____

3.2 What would you say to a person who says that they have not done anything wrong?

_____
_____
_____

3.3 Who can bring us near to God?

_____
_____
_____

3.4 What heart condition do we need for salvation, and explain what this consists of.

_____
_____
_____

3.5 What does someone who wants to receive blessings from God have to do?

_____
_____

4. What four things should we emphasise in verifying salvation?

_____
_____
_____
_____
_____
_____

5. Which two of the following four statements are correct?

   a) Allocation is done by considering various pieces of information with a view to opening a cell in that area.
   b) Allocation is done by looking for the cell meeting nearest to where the new believer lives.
   c) Allocation is done at random.
   d) Allocation is done according to the interests of the chosen group.

6. Write down the three purposes of the phone call.

   _____
   _____
   _____
   _____

7. What are the three most important things to think about when preparing for the phone call?

   _____
   _____
   _____
   _____
   _____
   _____

8. Tick the following statements that you consider to be successful phone call strategies:

   a) Be pleasant.
   b) Do not be impatient when praying, or finish the prayer too hastily.
   c) Do not take any more time than necessary.
   d) Do not put pressure on the new believer.
   e) Phone them during meal or rest times.

   "And whatever you do, do it heartily, as to the Lord and not to men" Colossians 3:23

THE HOME VISIT

THE HOME VISIT

Jesus knew how important it was to visit others. That's why He took the time to teach about it. In Matthew 8:14–15 we see how the Master Himself visited the house of Peter's mother–in–law. He prayed for her and healed her of a fever.

Then in Luke 19:1–10, Jesus went to the house of Zaccheus. After His visit, Zaccheus did not continue to do what he had been doing before. He showed genuine repentance.

The visits Jesus made to the house of Mary, Martha and Lazarus were very special. He was so friendly with the family that others commented about how much Jesus loved Lazarus (John 11:36).

Visiting homes was an extremely important mission for Jesus. He trained His disciples in it. Then He sent them out in twos to put it into practice (Mark 6:7-11). Even after He ascended into Heaven He continued to look for people who would continue and develop this work. That is why He chose Ananias and sent him to visit the home where Saul was staying.

With all this in mind, I want to challenge you to make home visits part of your lifestyle. It should be as normal for us as going to church. We need to motivate ourselves to commit to God and obey Him as Ananias did, overcoming any fear, inhibition or prejudices — whether intellectual, social, cultural or to do with age.

Visiting every single person that God puts into our hands will bring about the same results as Ananias's visit to Saul. And we will be built up and strengthened by the Holy Spirit in both our cell meetings as well as our church meetings. This is the key to success!

If you want to become a multiplier, become interested in people. When you visit a new believer who has just received Christ, you are not winning a soul but a friend – and maybe also a family and a new venue for a cell group.

THE PURPOSE OF THE HOME VISIT

1 To find out what their impression was about the meeting they attended at church.

To find out their needs and to minister to them under the guidance of the Holy Spirit. **2**

3 To link them to a cell group, and encourage them to get involved in the church activities, especially to go on an Encounter.

HOW TO PREPARE FOR THE VISIT

1 Contact the person, explain the reason for the visit and pray for them.

2 Confirm the day and time of the visit.

3 Think about, and prepare, something relevant to share with them. This should be based on the need recorded on the Verification form and on the phone call record.

4 Meet with the person who is going to accompany you. Pray together to receive God's support.

MAKING THE VISIT

When visiting, someone else should always accompany you. Jesus sent the 12 and the 70 out in twos to go home-visiting (Matthew 10:5–15; Luke 10:1).

Once you are at the house,
you should proceed in the following manner:

1 INTRODUCE YOURSELVES
If you do not know the person, introduce yourself and your companion, and try to be kind and sincere.

2 FIND OUT WHERE THEY ARE SPIRITUALLY
Ask how they felt in the Church meeting. Also talk with them about their specific problems and the reasons for them.

3 SHARE

Share with them. Minister to their needs with the Word of God, which contains examples of all the most common problems that people face. Show them how the light of the Bible can help meet their needs, and explain the biblical passage you have already prepared. This should take about ten minutes and should aim to impart to them faith in God.

4 PRAY

Pray specifically according to their need. Also minister to them in prayer – using the names of God, appropriate biblical promises, or those biblical verses that are able to touch the heart of the new believer. Avoid religious jargon during the prayer and be as natural as possible.

5 INVOLVE

Talk about church activities and encourage them to go. This is a good opportunity to create in them an awareness of the need to go to a cell meeting. Also encourage them to go on an Encounter.

6 RELEASE PEACE

Finish praying for the new believer and their family by releasing blessings and God's peace over their lives.

The chances of keeping a new believer are twice as great when he has been to two meetings at the Church, than when he has only been to one.

DURING THE VISIT

1. Introduce yourself

2. Investigate

3. Share

4. Pray

5. Involve

6. Release Peace

Pay great attention to new believers by visiting them promptly. This ensures that you will secure them much quicker for Christ.

"And I will give them eternal life, and they shall never perish; neither shall anyone snatch them out of My hand. My Father, who has given them to Me, is greater than all; and no one is able to snatch them out of My Father's hand".

John 10:28-29

MINISTER TO THEIR NEEDS
WITH THE WORD

1 TO THEIR MIND

- Renewing the mind (Romans 12:2)
- Taking thoughts captive (2 Corinthians 10:3–5)

2 TO THEIR HEART

- Feelings (Proverbs 4:23; 2 Timothy 2:22)
- Fear (1 John 4:18; Hebrews 13:5)
- Depression (Jeremiah 33:3;
  Matthew 11:28; Hebrews13:5)

3 TO THEIR SPIRIT

- Confession and repentance (1 John 1:9; Acts 3:19)
- Spiritual growth (Ephesians 2:20–22;
  2 Peter 1:5–8)

4 TO THEIR BODY

- Health (Isaiah 5:5; Mark 16:17–18)
- Temple of the Holy Spirit
  (1 Corinthians 6:18–20;
  2 Corinthians 6:16)

5 .TO THEIR RELATIONSHIPS

- With the family (Ephesians 5:21; 6:4)
- With other people (Ephesians 6:5–9; Titus 2:3–5)
- Restoration (Ecclesiastes 4:15; Isaiah 43:18)
- Forgiveness (Matthew 5:21–26; Ephesians 6:12)

6 TO THEIR FINANCES

- Prosperity through tithing (Malachi 3:10–12; Matthew 23:23)
- Freedom from financial ruin (Galatians 3:13; Genesis 3:17)
- Wisdom for handling money (James 1:5)
- Prosperity through giving (Luke 6:38)

Minister through Prayer

USE THE NAMES OF GOD ACCORDING TO THEIR NEEDS

Jeremiah 23:6
Jehovah Tsidkenu
The Lord our Righteousness
Ask God to establish His
righteousness and integrity in
their life as a fruit of knowing

Exodus 31:13
Jehovah M'Kaddesh
The Lord who Sanctifies
Pray that the Lord will sanctify
them in spirit, soul and mind
(1 Thessalonians 5:23).

Judges 6:24
Jehovah Shalom
The Lord my Peace
Claim the Peace of God that passes
all understanding and pray that this
will keep their hearts and mind in
Christ Jesus **(Philippians 4:9).**

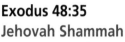

Exodus 48:35
Jehovah Shammah
The Lord who is Present
Pray for the presence of the Lord in their
daily life and in everything that they do.

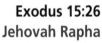

Exodus 15:26
Jehovah Rapha
The Lord my Healer
Declare that God heals every
sickness because by His wounds
we were healed
Isaiah 53:5.
Pray and release their healing.

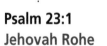

Genesis 22:13–14
Jehovah Jireh
The Lord my Provider
Ask God to supply everything they
need according to His riches in glory
Philippians 4:19.

Psalm 23:1
Jehovah Rohe
The Lord my Shepherd
Confess that God protects, looks
after and guides their lives.

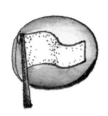

Exodus 17:15
Jehovah Nissi
The Lord my Banner
Ask for deliverance from the enemy
according to **Isaiah 59:19.** Declare that if
the enemy comes like a flood, the Lord will
raise up a standard against him.

Isaiah 1:3
Jehovah Sabaoth
The Lord of Hosts
Declare that all the power of
Heaven is available to meet
their needs.

Exodus 15:26
Jehovah Shaddai
The Lord Almighty
Confess that the Lord is the one
who emboldens, consoles,
strengthens and empowers them.

The purpose of the visit is to impart to the new believer the vision of the Church. It is also to involve them in church activities suitable for their age group, and the time they have available.

The leader must integrate the new believers he has visited into a cell meeting where the discipleship process can continue. This will also create friendships and give them the sense of belonging required for them to persevere in the Christian life.

ENSURING THE SUCCESS OF THE VISIT

1 Take care of your personal appearance and remember that you are an ambassador of God and his church (2 Corinthians 5:20).

- Be smart and clean and make sure you have fresh breath (Hebrews 10:22).

2 Knock on the door in a natural way. When the door opens, greet them politely.

3 Speak and listen.

- Talk instead of preaching, so that the new believer will feel free to join in.

- Avoid exaggerated body language.

- Do not contradict the partner who accompanies you as this may give a bad impression to the new believer.

- Do not talk at the same time or interrupt your partner

4 Go only at the agreed time.

- If you are in a hurry, it is better to postpone the visit. Make sure you agree a revised day and time.

  - It is not good to visit at meal times.

    - Leave a leaflet or literature with the person you are visiting..

REVISION

THE HOME VISIT

OBJECTIVE
To explain the things that are involved in a home visit for both the visitor as well as the new believer.

Read **Acts 9:1–31** and then answer the following questions:

1. THE ENCOUNTER

1.1 By what name did Saul call Jesus? (v.5)

_____

_____

_____

1.2 What was Saul's emotional and physical condition following his encounter with Jesus? (v.9)

_____

_____

_____

In the same way, people who give their lives to Jesus for the first time will recognise Him as their Lord and a reverent fear of God's sovereignty will be awakened in them.

2. THE CALL

2.1 What was God's command to Ananias? (v.10 and 12)

_____

_____

_____

_____

2.2 What was Ananias's response to the call? (v. 13 & 14)

_____
_____
_____
_____
_____

Regardless of the excuses we might have when God calls us to do something, we must understand that it is God Himself who is sending us, and is going with us, because He has a special purpose for us.

3. THE VISIT

3.1 What did Ananias do?

_____
_____
_____
_____
_____
_____

3.2 What happened to Saul when Ananias prayed for him? (v.18 & 19)

_____
_____
_____
_____
_____
_____

We can be sure that God does not differentiate between people and, just as God did for Ananias when he visited Saul, He will also do for us. It will be much more than we can ask or imagine, because His power is working in us as **Ephesians 3:20 teaches.**

4. THE RESULT

4.1 What did Saul do (v.20)?

_____

_____

_____

_____

_____

4.2 What happened to the churches as a result
of this visit?

_____

_____

_____

_____

_____

4.3 How did Paul apply this to his ministry? **Acts 15:36**

_____

_____

_____

_____

_____

_____

_____

_____

A person won for the Lord through a visit is capable of
changing entire nations by telling of what God has
done in them:
**"...from Jerusalem and round about to Illyricum I
have fully preached the gospel of Christ."** Romans
15:19. So lets go for it!

SHORT SERMONS

"And my speech and my preaching were not with persuasive words of human wisdom, but in demonstration of the Spirit and of power".
1 Corinthians 2:4

SHORT SERMONS

One of the most important things that determines the success of the visit is the short sermon you will share with the new believer while you are there. For this reason you have to prepare the passage well and seek guidance from the Holy Spirit as to which scripture will meet their need. Study and meditate on that scripture.

1 Corinthians 2 gives us several words of
advice about sharing the Word.

1. Don't go with words of human wisdom, but rather
with demonstration of the Holy Spirit's power.
Moreover, don't preach to show your own eloquence
or to win the applause of people. Rather, present God
as alive and real, capable of changing all things
because He has the power to do so.

2. Go in fear and trembling. Go totally dependent
upon God, knowing that everything we say and do is
from Christ, not from us. It is not through our ability
but through God's mercy.

3. Seek the guidance of the Holy Spirit. He is the
only One who knows the heart of the new
believer. It is He who can reveal to us deep
things about them, so that we can touch
their lives with the power of God.
The short sermons most appropriate for a
home visit are those based on either a text or
theme. Where a text is used, it will be a verse
or a short passage of Scripture.
The text chosen must be clear, direct and
easily applied to the new believer's need.
Note, however, that this is not the time or
place to use interpretations outside of the
text itself or turn it into a detailed Bible study.

Your short sermon should be taken from a few verses relevant to the person's need and explained within ten minutes. You should emphasise how it will influence their life, how it will bring new meaning to them and how it will offer answers to their particular situations.

The simpler the message, the better the results will be. Always use the Bible as the authority for your explanations and counsel.

As far as possible, use practical or personal examples that will help your listener to develop their faith. Make sure your objectives are clear, and do not let anything side-track you from them.

Prepare a number of short sermons on the most common topics such as family, healing, spiritual condition or finances. These can then be adjusted, once you have prayed, to the need of each individual believer. They must be simple, practical, and centred on Christ.

Be positive and never condemn. Rather give encouragement, inspire faith, bring about restoration, and don't forget to introduce the crux of the gospel, which is genuine repentance.

Always edify and build up faith in your listener, emphasising that we are children of a God who loves us, who wants to bless us, heal us and develop us. Avoid any criticism or accusation that will create a negative response in your listener rather than motivating or encouraging them. Remember: a conversation that fails to show the love of God and inspire faith, does not build life in the new believer, nor does it encourage them to follow Jesus.

Conclude by inviting the new believer to put into practice all that he or she has learned, and by motivating them to do it. Demonstrate to them the benefits of obedience, listening to God's advice, and daring to find out that He will never disappoint those who trust in Him.

Remember	**IN YOUR**
You have the power of God to do this work and that is why He chose and sent you. Believe in God. He does not send anyone out to fail. He will support you, He will use you, and there will be many who will tell of God's wonders, thanks to your obedience and attitude.	**PREACHING:**
	Build up
	Impart faith
	Encourage
	Motivate
	Restore

I have included in this book some examples of short sermons which might help you on your first visit.

FEAR

OBJECTIVE

To motivate people with all kinds of fears to trust in the Lord as their source of help.

1. Fear begins when we stray from God, as seen in Genesis 3:8–10. When we fail, fear comes into our lives, and this kind of mistake spoils our relationship with God.

2. Fear starts to limit our abilities (Proverbs 29:25). Fear will cause you to miss out on opportunities, to be negative and to think that everything is impossible. The solution is to begin to trust God again.

3. How to restore the presence of God in our life.

    a. Receive Jesus into your heart (confirm the salvation of the new believer).

  b. Accept and believe the fact that Jesus is with you. (Hebrews 13:5-6). Only the presence of God will remove every fear. His presence brings us strength, value and faith, and takes away every negative thought.

COMMENTARY

Encourage the new believer not to let negative thinking dominate them. Motivate them to confess that now they are in Jesus, He will go before them and no evil will come to them. Pray with them, emphasising the fact that Jesus is in them and that He will remain with them.

"There is no fear in love; but perfect love casts out fear, because fear involves torment. But he who fears has not been made perfect in love".
1 John 4:18.

SPIRITUAL GROWTH

OBJECTIVE

To teach the new believer what he or she needs to do in order to grow in their Christian life.

"For this very reason, giving all diligence, add to your faith virtue, to virtue knowledge, and to knowledge self control, to self control perseverance, to perseverance godliness, to godliness brotherly kindness, and to brotherly kindness love. For if these things are yours and abound, you will be neither barren nor unfruitful in the knowledge of our Lord Jesus Christ."

2 Peter 1:5–8.

1. Talk to the new believer about their need to be a disciple and not merely a church-goer. Explain that being a disciple means to follow Christ obediently every day.

2. Teach them to spend time reading the Bible each day, beginning with the New Testament. Teach them to meditate on what has been read, asking these three questions:

   a. What does this tell me about God? (His personality, character, attributes)

   b. What is He commanding me to do? What does God want me to do in obedience to Him?

   c. What is God promising me? Which promises is the Lord inviting me to claim today?

3. Teach the new believer to pray to God in a conversational way. The prayer should be both spontaneous and sincere.

Explain the various aspects of prayer, such as worship, petition, confession and intercession.

COMMENTARY

Encourage the new believer to start on a daily discipline of reading the Bible, meditating on it and praying. Even if it is only for fifteen minutes at the outset, this will be a good start for every new believer. Pray for this person so that they see how to do it, and allow them the opportunity to join in if they wish to.

"For if these things are yours and abound, you will be neither barren nor unfruitful in the knowledge of our Lord Jesus."
2 Peter 1:8

FAMILY PROBLEMS

OBJECTIVE

To challenge the new believer to overcome all obstacles to family reconciliation.

1. Every family problem brings tension to members of the family and creates an environment of conflict and insecurity.

2. It is necessary to forgive in order to bring Christ's presence into the home. Matthew 5:21–26.

3. Overcoming pride and taking the first step towards reconciliation is a true Christian act which is pleasing to God. At the same time we are receiving the forgiveness that God offers us.
Matthew 18:32–35.

4. Teach them that prayer can help us to give ground and to change.

COMMENTARY

We should not try to force others into reconciliation. It is better to allow the Holy Spirit to work in each person.

Pray for each family member, that a spirit of forgiveness, restoration and love will come upon them.

Wherever possible, look for a way in which the offended person can pray for and bless the one who hurt them, as this will bring genuine forgiveness.

If you conquer your pride you will take the first step to achieve reconciliation

DEPRESSION

OBJECTIVE
To bring hope to the person, to renew their thoughts and help them to leave things in the hands of God.

1. Depression is a state of mind that causes people to see everything around them in a negative way. They experience feelings of sadness, failure, rejection, and lose sight of reality. They are overwhelmed by a feeling that God has abandoned them.

2. You must show that person that they are not alone. Take them to Hebrews 13:5 and emphasise the fact that God is with them and that they should seek Him.

3. Encourage them to renew their mind (Romans 12:2). Changing their way of thinking will enable them to see the marvellous plans that God has for their life.

4. Invite them to cast their cares on to Jesus (Matthew 11:28). It is His desire that we give Him all our worries so that we can find our rest in Him.

5. The prayer must be a confession of victory, a declaration of the excellent things God has for us and must emphasise how much God loves us and believes in us.

COMMENTARY

Encourage the new believer not to let their problems oppress them. Encourage them to trust in Jesus and to bring all their feelings and problems to Him. Pray with them emphasising God's Sovereignty and the fact that God is in control of all things.

"...be transformed by the renewing of your mind".

Romans 12:2

DIVINE GUIDANCE

OBJECTIVE

To teach the new believer how to receive godly guidance and how to make decisions.

1. God is the fountain of all wisdom and He gives it to His children. Proverbs 2:6-7 says that every decision we make will shape our future.

2. We must trust in God's direction and not in our own understanding (Proverbs 3 :5–8).
The Word of God has the answer for all our worries and the Holy Spirit brings conviction to our heart when we truly desire to submit to His leading.

3. We must obey God's advice. Jesus was the model of perfect obedience to His Father in everything, and because of this He is the friend and helper of all who obey Him (John 15:10 & 14).

4. Seeking and obeying God's advice always brings blessing. Proverbs 3:13–18 shows that gaining wisdom is more profitable and beneficial than attaining any material things, wealth, honour, peace and joy, or living to a ripe old age.

COMMENTARY

Emphasise how God guides and reveals His direction to all who sincerely desire to obey Him. Encourage the new believer to read the Bible, to search for answers and to pray to the Holy Spirit to bring peace into their heart. When you pray, confess that God has complete control over your situation and accept His will, believing that He has the best in store for you.

> "Trust in the Lord with all your heart,
> and lean not on your own
> understanding."
> **Proverbs 3:5**

FINANCES

OBJECTIVE

To encourage the new believer to trust in God to take care of all their needs.

1. God, by His nature, is a giver and a provider. Explain each of God's names, by which we might know something of His character. One of His names is Jehovah Jireh, which signifies that He is by nature our provider (Genesis 22:14).

2. The curse of financial poverty began with the fall of man (Genesis 3:17–19). Explain that as we have all failed God, the curse of financial poverty has been passed down from Adam to all men.

3. Christ has redeemed us from the curse of the law (Galatians 3:13–14). When Christ died on the cross, the crown of thorns symbolised that He was carrying the curse of Genesis 3:17. Therefore today when we accept Him in our lives (confirm their salvation at this point), we are freed from the curse of poverty.

4. God promises to supply all our needs. He commits to provide for all who are His children and who obey Him.

COMMENTARY

Encourage the person to believe in the sufficiency of the death of Christ to redeem them, and that He desires to give them all they need. Invite them to begin to pray every day specifically for their needs. Tell them that, when praying they need to pray in the name of Jehovah Jireh and then give thanks to God for the answer.

"Christ has redeemed us from the curse of the law, having become a curse for us (for it is written 'Cursed is everyone that is hung on a tree')".
Galatians 3:13

HEALING

OBJECTIVE

To get the sick person to the point where they believe that Jesus took their sickness and that He can heal them.

1. Sickness is not God's purpose (John 10:10). Explain that God does not like to see His sons and daughters sick. On the contrary, He desires to heal them so that they can enjoy abundant life.

2. Jesus came to die on the cross to give us salvation (confirm salvation in the new believer at this point) and also to carry our sicknesses in His body (Isaiah 53:4). When Christ died on the cross, He also established freedom from infirmity for us. Therefore, He has the power to heal those who believe in Him.

3. Jesus' promise to us is this: if we believe, we will lay hands on sick people and they will get well. We should explain that our hands are nothing special – it is Jesus that heals through our touch (Mark 16:17–18).

COMMENTARY

Do not be afraid to pray over the telephone: Isaiah 53:4-5 and Exodus 15:26.
Make sure the person you are talking to believes in Christ and has decided to obey Him.

"Surely He has borne our griefs (sicknesses) and carried our sorrows (pains)"
Isaiah 53:4

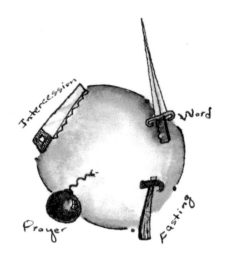

How To Overcome Temptation

OBJECTIVE

To give the new believer the tools needed to overcome troubles and sin, and to live in victory.

"No temptation has overtaken you except such as is common to man; and God is faithful, who will not allow you be tempted beyond what you are able, but with the temptation will also make the way of escape, that you may be able to bear it."

1 Corinthians 10:13.

1. God knows us and He will never let us receive any temptation that is too great for us to resist.

2. God provides us with a way of escape from temptation.

3. Because Christ was tempted Himself and overcame it, He is there with us when we are tempted and is able to help us also to overcome it.

COMMENTARY

Encourage the new believer to acknowledge their weaknesses honestly, and to ask for God's help because He is our only source of help.

Encourage them to spend time doing things that will strengthen their spiritual life (studying and reading the Bible, prayer, helping in church). Point out to them all the things they can lose if they give in to temptation.

"...God is faithful, who will not allow you be tempted beyond what you are able, but with the temptation will also make the way of escape, that you may be able to bear it."

1 Corinthians 10:13

REJECTION

OBJECTIVE

To show the new believer that rejection is a trick of the enemy, and to demonstrate that God accepts them unconditionally.

1. Rejection is a feeling that you are inferior to other people, and that you have no value.

2. Rejection causes shyness which leads to isolation, poor relationships and fear of other people.

3. It is important to show the new believer just how valuable he or she is to God. Ephesians 1:3–14 shows how God blesses us and wants the best for us, how He wants to adopt us as His children, forgiving us, and loving us in spite of everything.

COMMENTARY

Encourage the new believer not to believe things that people have said about them in the past. Rather encourage them to believe what God says about them, and to understand their adoption as a child of God and the real value God places on them.

COURTSHIP

OBJECTIVE

To make the new believer aware of the importance of courtship, of making decisions about courtship, and the role of courtship as a preparation towards marriage.

1. God loves you and wants the best for you.
   "For I know the thoughts that I think towards you, says the Lord, thoughts of peace and not of evil, to give you a future and a hope." Jeremiah 29:11

   There is no one that knows you better than God. He knows exactly the type of person who is best suited to your character, and He will give him or her to you.

2. God knows your heart, and He knows better than you do who will be the best partner for you.

"For the Lord does not see as man sees; for man looks at the outward appearance, but the Lord looks at the heart." 1 Samuel 16:7.

By far the best and safest way of choosing the right person is to seek the guidance of the One who knows our hearts. Our own wisdom can fail us, but God does not make mistakes.

3. Courtship is a preparation for marriage. For this reason we should be very careful about who we give our hearts and affection to.
"Keep your heart with all diligence, for out of it spring the issues of life." Proverbs 4:23.

COMMENTARY

Lead the person to commit his emotional life into the hands of the Lord, seeking His direction until He gives them an answer. Encourage the person to ask God if the person they are friends with is the right person for them. Get them to ask God to develop a close spiritual harmony between them if the person is right for them to marry and, if not, for Him to take away their peace. If the person is not right, tell them to ask God to give them the boldness and determination to end the relationship.

God knows your heart and the person who is best for you.

OBJECTIONS

OBJECTIONS

During the consolidation process with the new believers, they may throw up objections to the Word of God which will hinder them in their relationship with Him.

1 Peter 3:15 says "But sanctify the Lord God in your hearts, and always be ready to give a defence to everyone who asks you a reason for the hope that is in you, with meekness and fear".

The Apostle Peter gives good advice. Always be prepared to explain to those who ask the reason for the hope you have – in other words the reason for your faith in the Lord Jesus Christ.

That preparation includes knowing your doctrine so that you can explain it wisely when asked.

Give your answers with wisdom and in meekness, without anger or arguing, but with reverence, with respect for the other person, listening to their point of view, and without even a hint of arrogance. Through such behaviour the love of God will be genuinely shown, and will disarm those speaking against Christianity.

2 Tim 2:24–26 says:
"And a servant of the Lord must not quarrel but be gentle to all, able to teach, patient, in humility correcting those who are in opposition, if God perhaps will grant them repentance, so that they may know the truth".

"But sanctify the Lord God in your hearts, and always be ready to give a defence to everyone who asks you a reason for the hope that is in you, with meekness and fear."
1 Peter 3:15

Characteristics which you should display when dealing with those who oppose you:

1. Don't be contentious

2. Be kind

3. Be able to teach

4. Be patient

5. Be gentle

In 1 Peter 3:15 we see various characteristics that the servant of God should display when dealing with those who oppose him:

1. DO NOT BE CONTENTIOUS.

As it says in verse 23, do not fight with others because of their faith. Avoid foolishly probing into issues that will cause argument. The purpose is not to win a discussion, but to win that life to Christ, or at least to leave the door open for new opportunities when God works in their lives.

2. BE KIND TO ALL.

Always respond in tenderness and love, irrespective of their reactions, remembering that our fight is not against flesh and blood, but against the powers of darkness (Ephesians 6:12).

Your polite and kind behaviour will give them more confidence to talk to you and to share with you their deep-rooted beliefs.

3. BE ABLE TO TEACH.

As well as knowing the Word of God, an ability to communicate it to others is required, applying it skilfully to their situation. We need to have the answers to the questions and objections which might crop up, and be able to respond to them wisely.

4. BE PATIENT.

Speak without any hint of resentment, and be tolerant and patient in the face of opposition and insult.

5. GENTLY CORRECT THOSE WHO OPPOSE YOU.

You will only persuade people with objections if you are meek. Be sure to avoid any hint of anger, and be aware that correction means to overcome the arguments and objections that exist in their minds, thereby freeing them from wrong thinking and leading them to the truth.

The purpose of this correction is to bring them to repentance so that they will escape from the snares of the enemy.

THE SOURCE OF OBJECTIONS

The best way to confront objections is to understand their source. Once you know this, it will help you to overcome them.

For example, there is a great increase in the number of sects in our society today. One result of involvement in a sect is a fear and mistrust of any belief other than that which has been taught by the sect.

There are also other factors such as people's problems or previous events that have separated them from God. They may have developed prejudices through coming across believers who say one thing, and do the opposite.

Another influence is the rule of Satan. He knows how to bring spiritual blindness and confuse the understanding of those who do not know God. He also uses other tools such as doubt, fear and confusion.

HOW TO HANDLE OBJECTIONS

1. CONQUER THEM IN THE SPIRITUAL REALM.

Before you do anything, win the battle in the spiritual realm through prayer. Break down the fortress and demolish the arguments in the mind of the person who has objected. In other words, pull down all prejudices and opinions which they believe to be true and which hinder them from accepting the Word of God (2 Corinthians 10:45).

2. LISTEN WITH PATIENCE.

Pay close attention to what the person is saying, without interrupting them. This will inspire them to reveal the deep thoughts of their hearts. At the same time, it will give them more confidence to express the reasons for their opposition.

3. SEARCH FOR THE SPECIFIC OBJECTION.

Try to discover the specific objections and prejudices which are keeping the person from God. You need to uncover them in order to be able to refute them in the light of the Bible.

4. SATURATE YOUR ANSWER WITH THE WORD OF GOD.

John 8:32 says "And you will know the truth, and the truth shall make you free". For this reason every excuse, however innocent it may be, must be challenged in the light of the Scriptures. Remember, it is through lack of knowledge that the people perish. "My people are destroyed for lack of knowledge" Hosea 4:6.

Do not let anything discourage them or distract them from the purpose of God, irrespective of what other people say or think. Maintain a heart full of love for them, seeing them as God sees them in the light of salvation and freedom.

WHAT TO DO IN THE FACE OF AN OBJECTION

1. First win the victory in the spiritual realm

2. Listen patiently

3. Search for the specific objection

4. Saturate your response with the Word of God

They may have had experiences in the past with people calling themselves believers who are not, which are preventing them from receiving the Word of God.

Satan plays his part by bringing spiritual blindness, fear and confusion.

FREQUENT EXCUSES
AND HOW TO OVERCOME THEM

When you present the gospel, it is possible
that you will come across people who are not
interested in listening to anything you say. It is
necessary to uncover the reasons behind their
reaction, and to learn how to deal with excuses
when they arise.

Colossians 4:5–6 says:
"Walk in wisdom toward those who are
outside, redeeming the time. Let your speech
always be with grace, seasoned with salt, that
you may know how you ought to answer each
one."

Our words are reinforced by the wisdom we
show in dealing with non–believers. In other
words, we should be a good witness to all who
do not yet know God. If you are not, they will
not be ready to receive what you are sharing
with them.

The Holy Spirit is guiding us to speak the Word
of God with grace. This is what will open
people's hearts to listen and create in them the
desire to obey God.

It is important to give the Word of God in the right measure. Do not give them too much so that they will become weary of it, nor give them too little so that they will not be able to grasp what you are saying. The point is to give your listener a word that will benefit their lives, causing them to believe for themselves, and giving them a desire to behave correctly.

It is therefore necessary to have grace and a word in season, to be able to answer every objection, and to clarify things in such a way that their minds will be touched by the word of God, and all prejudice, self–sufficiency and apathy removed. Their hearts will turn to God and they will live a life that pleases Him.

"For I will give you a mouth and wisdom that which all your adversaries will not be able to contradict or resist."
Luke 21:15

Do not be afraid! When you share the Word, the Holy Spirit will give you grace, hearts will be touched and arguments against the gospel pulled down.

To do this in an informal way requires preparation. Part of that preparation is to understand the frequent reasons that harden people against the things of God. For this reason, we need to find answers that will make people aware of their true condition, and of their need of Christ.

Some of the most frequent excuses that arise when you telephone the new believer, or when you try to get them involved in the church, are as follows:

1. I DON'T HAVE TIME…
Usually, they give many different reasons for their lack of time, but what they are really saying is that God isn't that important to them. Even though they may say the opposite, they will find that they have more time if they make God a priority.

2. I AM NOT INTERESTED BECAUSE…
Although this objection can appear disappointing, it can come from a person eager for God, but who doesn't want to accept that he needs Him. In this situation, the skill of the consolidator can demolish many arguments and lead the person to become a committed believer.

3. I WOULD LIKE TO, BUT I CAN'T BECAUSE...
When a new believer comes into the church there
are issues to resolve. There will definitely be
situations that have impacted them, and left
certain feelings in their lives. Behind the statement
'I would like to, but I haven't decided yet', there
are usually fears and arguments in their minds
which cause them to have a negative attitude to
Christianity. The important thing here is to listen to
them and try and find out the real reason why they
don't want to stay and take the opportunity to
know God. Once we discover this, we can use the
Word of God to counter their arguments and show
them that their fear is unfounded.

One of the most efficient methods of learning how
to refute objections is to study the Word of God in
a personal way. For this reason I have included in
this book the biblical answers to these kinds of
objections. However, do some further work on this
yourself, so that you feel confident you have found
the best answers.

THE MOST FREQUENT OBJECTIONS	1. I don't have time 2. I am not interested because... 3. I would like to, but I cannot because...

 **REVISION**

OBJECTIONS

OBJECTIVE
To learn to handle the different excuses and objections through Bible study.

2 Timothy 2:15 says:
"Be diligent to present yourself approved to God, a worker who does not need to be ashamed, rightly dividing the word of truth."

To be able to respond to the different types of excuses and objections you will need to be persistent in your preparation if you are to succeed.

Find Scriptures that will help you to respond to the following objections:

1. **I DON'T HAVE TIME...**
   a) I have only got time for my job, or my studies.
   b) It is not important to set aside time for God, when you can do something that is more fun.
   c) It is not necessary to go to church to be with God. You only have to offer Him what you do.

2. **I AM NOT INTERESTED BECAUSE...**
   a) Being a Christian is very difficult.
   b) My family and friends are against it.
   c) I don't want to change my religion.
   d) I don't believe in God.
   e) I have heard that you ask for money or tithes.

3. **I WANT TO, BUT I DON'T GO BECAUSE...**
   a) There are no images.
   b) I want to enjoy life first.
   c) There are still some things I don't understand.
   d) I don't know anybody.
   e) There are so many hypocrites.

Match the following scriptures with the nine statements below.

1 Corinthians 6:12   **Matthew 6:33**
Romans 5:8   **Ecclesiastes 12:1**
John 14:6   **Proverbs 16:25**
Exodus 23:2   **Hebrews 9:27**
John 7:17

1. I try to be as good as I can,
    and I believe God accepts me. _____

2. Christianity is very complicated and
    the demands are great._____

3. Perhaps I will have another opportunity
    after death. _____

4. I am too young
    to follow Christ._____

5. There is no way out for me;
    I have been too bad and
    God will never forgive me. _____

6. I never do anyone any harm,
    and I do not have anything
    to repent of._____

7. It could all be
    a big mistake._____

8. I believe there are
    many ways to God. _____

9. I cannot leave my friends.

    _____